ISBN: 9798810555841

Imprint: Independently published

Welcome To You All

The Heightened Risks Of Human Extinction.

Intensified risk and actual use of Weapons of Mass Destruction [WMDs] brought by advanced technological advancement nevertheless concealed digital WMDs are being used and the political climate where Nato's article 5 gives immunity to countries breaking international laws regarding weapons of mass destruction.

Nato's expansion and their blanket protection to all kinds of evil using article 5 and the intense political climate where other countries have to match the force and threat at hand in Nato led them to make even more destructive weapons in nukes. The current war is proof of how thin a line it is between extinction and humanity's survival.

WE CAN'T LEAVE THINGS TO CHANCE.

Ladies and gentlemen, boys and girls, welcome to Tomorrow's World Order. We are now fully operational with immediate effect.

Signed

24 April 2022

Founder and President Tomorrow's World Order

David Gomadza

00447745900178

www.twocoming.com

Tomorrowsworldorder@outlook.com
A New World Order

Tomorrow's World Order
Official Strategic Launch
www.twocoming.com
tomorrowsworldorder@outlook.com
00447745900178

To:

The Russian and Ukrainian Governments
Mr Presidents
STOP THE WAR NOW.
Only you two have the power to do so.

We are deeply concerned with the huge loss of lives. As a matter of urgency and emergency, we call for the **immediate cessation of the conflict, loss of lives, deteriorating humanitarian situation, and the immediate start of negotiations in order to reach a peaceful and lasting soluti**on.

The good news is that there is a solution to the conflict. Through us, you can start immediate negotiations that lead to peace. We provide a platform and environment for peace and sound fruitful negotiations that lead to diplomatic, sustainable resolutions.

We are the new global leaders, peacekeepers, negotiators, mediators, facilitators, and defenders of the defenceless mainly women and children, among other things.

We strongly believe that the lack of a proper plaftorm to encourage dialogue, diplomacy, negotiations and the mistrust of the current system is the sole reason why this escalated into this conflict.

We know the system is not what it seems. The current system is broken, dysfunctional and honestly not fit for purpose. Surely we strongly believe that if proper channels of negotiations were available. Channels trusted by both of you Mr Presidents. Surely the conflict could have been resolved in a diplomatic way through dialogue.

We therefore take this opportunity to introduce a new world order that means peace for all.

There is hope for an amicably diplomatic resolution to the conflict.

We therefore require the immediate cessation of this conflict and the immediate cessation of hostilities and the immediate start of dialogue without any preconditions.

You must fully comply with our requirements for we stand for all.

We are neutral and represent all humanity.

We know the current system let you all down but there is hope. We are the future. It is not too late to reach a peaceful and lasting solution to the crisis.

START PEACE NEGOTIATIONS WITH IMMEDIATE EFFECT DIPLOMACY IS THE ONLY SOLUTION.

signed President Tomorrow's World Order 24 April 2022 David Gomadza.

Tomorrow's World Order

Official Strategic Launch

24 April 2022

As the new global leaders, overseers, negotiators, facilitators, mediators, intermediaries, defenders of the defenseless, peacekeepers, among other things.

To fill the huge gap in the current global justice system. The pandemic and the current war have highlighted serious critical shortfalls of the current system, especially in terms of defending women and children who end up dead due to wars. In stopping wars. In negotiating or in the provision of such a framework. In support of people who need assistance at a time of need, among other things.

David Gomadza

Founder & President

Tomorrow's World Order

SECTIONS

"The [international] law can be a double-edged sword to those who violate it and a source of hope, comfort, and inspiration to those who seek justice and peace."
— David Gomadza, Tomorrow's World Order

I

Overview

Critical issues that threaten the survival of all humanity at large have triggered the rise of Tomorrow's World Order hereby thereof abbreviated to TWO. Critical factors are so paramount to the survival of all humanity that it is mandatory that we rise as the negotiators, guardians, mediators, facilitators, and overseers of the world with immediate effect.

We have an obligation and responsibility to safeguard the existence of humanity. The current situation made it a critical issue that a power like us arises promptly to contain the situation.

Even though we anticipated this and prepared a framework to take over as global guardians and overseers in 2018. The recent developments and the two major issues at hand made it critical that we take over and start a new world order with immediate effect to stop the war from escalating.

The two situations are;

The rise of never seen concealed digital weapons of mass destruction; ones triggered by advanced technological development. The pandemic, which is the current reference point, is a critical point that can determine the existence or extinction of humanity.

The risk of an all-out nuclear war given rise by current political tensions and settings in which the Russian-Ukraine war is a reference point. This is evidence of the challenges and difficulties mankind faces today. Above all, the risk of extinction is fueled by this situation in which a country might feel threatened and feel insecure. Enough to make weapons of mass destruction as a direct response to the force and magnitude of the threat at hand. In that, a country like Russia might resort to nuclear weaponry as a means to counteract the threat posed by Nato in case they are attacked. Bearing in mind that Russia has more than 6000 nuclear warheads with Nato members having nearly equal nukes between them and the current tension surely requires the setting up of a new world order led by Tomorrow's World Order.

We are hereby announcing to the world the setting up of a new system of global governance, planning, and management led by Tomorrow's World Order. New world order and from hereby thereof we are the new world leaders to act in everyone's best interest. A new world order where we have the ability to stop wars and just do that. Every country, institution, cult, etc is obliged to acknowledge us as the new global leaders. All countries, cults, institutions, etc are answerable to us as we are neutral of any interest that is associated with cults, institutions, or nations. We have humanity's best interest; that is our main focus.

Tomorrow's World Order's President has the final say. The current system has crashed and is now obsolete. The current war is evidence of all this.

Our Roles as Global Leaders.

Put a platform to stop wars.

Intervene before wars start and encourage negotiations.

To put effective negotiating channels to be adhered to by all sides.

Control situations from escalating to dangerous levels.

Act as negotiators, facilitators, intermediaries, mediators, between nations.

Act as interpreters, updaters, formulators, and implementers of international laws in relation to the changing times.

Defenders of international laws regarding wars, invasions, and war crimes.

Defenders of ordinary citizens regarding wars, sanctions, etc.

Defenders of women and children.

Rewriters of international laws where it's unclear in relation to changing circumstances.

Enforcers of all international laws.

Vetting instruments of institutions, cults, nations, etc in terms of fit for purpose in relation to giving a false sense of security to ordinary people especially in terms of claims to stop the war. With institutions, cults, etc promising women and children peace, and life then let all the people down only for all to be killed.

Advisors to all during invasions, wars, sanctions, war crimes, etc.

Planning and management of global financial, economic, social, and political instruments on a global scale.

We have the right to command the international community to deal with violators of international laws based on the Hostis Humanis Generis principle. Any enemies of humanity. People, nations, cults, etc who use WMDs that threaten humanity's survival will be dealt with by anyone worldwide at our command. We have a license to order others to kill violators of international laws. Gone are the days we tolerate barbaric evil practices. No one is immune. We command others to shoot in broad daylight and on national television and put proof in our blockchain system for all to see.

Act as a recommendations board for things that can improve humanity at large.

Lead in discovering new advanced technological breakthroughs and take humanity to the next stage of development.

Your Obligations in relation to Tomorrow's World Order.

You must acknowledge us as the new global leaders. You are accountable to us in relation to international laws. We have everyone's interests.

You are all obliged to obey international laws and all our recommendations. You have an obligation to act within the framework of international laws. These laws are for everyone, you and future generations. We act in humanity's interest.

No one is immune in terms of breaches of international laws. One man or woman for him/herself and TWO for us all. It's your duty not to breach these laws.

Know what is expected of you in relation to international laws. Our system can judge people in absentia. Only real evil people will be trapped by our system. If you are clean, you have nothing to worry about.

Support us. Join us. No woman or child will ever die needlessly because of wars, sanctions, etc. Put yourself in the position of a woman or child who died. Imagine institutions claiming that they can stop wars. Imagine believing this and not acting or running believing they will stop wars. Imagine dying when you least expected simply because some distractors lied to you, to everyone that they can stop wars. Is that fair? To make things worse, currently, there is no one who can stop wars. NO ONE.

"You need to act immediately," Zelensky implored the UN Security Council during a live-streamed address on April 6 to its members.

"the next option would be to dissolve yourself altogether. And I know you can admit that if there is nothing you can do besides conversation.

Zelensky 6 April 2022.

Tomorrow's World Order. Dealing with the threats of invasion, wars, and war crimes. Page 23. [5 Feb 2020]

They stated that they can stop wars.

United Nations

"To save succeeding generations from the scourge of war" are among the first very words of the UN Charter (in its Preamble), and those words were the main motivation for creating the United Nations, whose founders had lived through the devastation of two world wars by 1945. Since the UN's creation on 24 October 1945 (the date its Charter came into force), the United Nations has often been called upon to prevent disputes from escalating into war, to help restore peace following the outbreak of armed conflict, and to promote lasting peace in societies emerging from wars.

Security Council

Over the decades, the UN has helped to end numerous conflicts, often through actions of the Security Council — the organ with primary responsibility, under the United Nations Charter, for the maintenance of international peace and security. When it receives a complaint about a threat to peace, the Council first recommends that the parties seek an agreement by peaceful means. In some cases, the Council itself investigates and mediates. It may appoint special representatives or request the Secretary-General to do so or to use his good offices. It may set forth principles for a peaceful settlement.

UN

One woman's or child's death is an attack on all of us. No more protecting evil with article 5 etc. A New World Order. Together, stronger. We stand for the women and children who are getting killed easily with no one to defend them.

Cooperate with us. We are not changing anything, just putting a framework to deal with international law violators. A better world for all.

II

Guiding Principles.

In part I, I will deal with the West's inadequacies as a trigger for the need for a new system, and a new setting for a new world order in TWO.

In part II, I will deal with other non-West countries, cults, institutions, etc as contributing to the need for a totally new way of doing things triggering the rise of TWO.

Part 1

I argued in Tomorrow's World Order [check last pages for details] that only a new system can solve today's problems. The current system was put in place to hold-in-place the current already crashed and obsolete system. All current systems no matter how harsh these sounds are put in place just to fuel wars; to distract the people who end up dead, facilitate wars and exonerate their founders in most cases the triggers of wars. This is partly true in the case of the United Nations Security Council, now referred to as UNSC. The current system uses weapons as the drivers of the economy. Where mankind has little money to buy resources he needs at fair market prices, resources such as oil. Mankind with the little money he has. He makes weapons and then uses the weapons to control the flow of money and lower the prices of resources by controlling supply and demand. All this through wars, sanctions, and all kinds of evil in the process killing women and children.

I want to point out that there is no justification whatsoever as technology has meant new alternatives in all areas be it energy or fuel, etc. All parts of the current system; the UNSC, the United Nations, Nato, etc are ineffective in stopping wars and above all in protecting the lives of children and women who end up dead. The ineffectiveness of these cults, institutions, etc gave rise to Tomorrow's World Order. Where there is a system crash only a new system is needed to replace the obsolete system. Hence our presence.

Our system will acknowledge the sovereignty of each nation. Meaning a right not to be attacked. There is no justification for invading other countries unless it is our direct command. So, forbidden.

Let me point out outright that we have powers to command all people, countries, cults, institutions, etc to attack a country that is breaching international laws. International laws are for the benefit of all humanity. They fall under the Jus Cogens laws that safeguard the existence of all humans regardless of race, religion, political orientation, age, gender, sexual orientation, etc,

Secondly, TWO will command a stronghold of two hundred lethal assassins who will blast anyone, a leader, president, prime minister, a queen, a king, etc who breaches international laws. No one is immune. We have laws that deal with culprits on an individual basis.

No one is immune to international laws. We will blast anyone in broad daylight and on national television if they breach international laws that are in the interest of everyone.

Why the rise of Tomorrow's World Order?

The ineffectiveness of the current system.

The current system was developed after the second world war just to hold-in-place an already collapsed obsolete system see explanations later in the book.

World development is in stages as I argued in my book Tomorrow's World Order. We are still stuck in the defensive stage of development where defense plays a crucial role in everything mankind does. In this stage, weapons are paramount and are the sole drivers of the economy. This is a fact even though the economy is believed to be a result of industrialization, manufacturing, technological advancement, etc. the underlying driver is the weapons. Where a huge budget is spent on the military, etc. But when there are no wars, the system is meant to fail as there is a huge stockpile of weapons and an imbalance as other areas suffer as all money is plowed into the military. That increases tension enough to cause the collapse of the system. Huge plowing of income into this military causes instability effects as other areas suffer at the expense. That creates tension.

But over the years it starts to make no sense to keep increasing budgets. This is the problem. Over time, everyone involved; presidents, prime ministers, kings, monarchies, queens, defense leaders, cults, institutions, etc will all become reluctant in stopping wars but actually wish for war. They will all see a relief point in the system. A perfect opportunity to offload weapons, revive their existence, revive their importance, etc. In that even if they could stop the war they won't stop the war. But instead, take the opportunity to help others like in the case of Ukraine to quell critics who accuse them of wastage. Now they can donate the weapons or make secret deals to feel good about themselves. In this case, they would not necessarily stop the war. Instead, they wait for an opportunity to make weapons deals, in an 'I scratch your back now so that you can scratch mine later.'

That means that the current system is ineffective in stopping wars.

[We have powers to judge all institutions, cults, nations, presidents, prime ministers, kings, queens, monarchies, etc.]

All current institutions, cults, power establishments, etc have failed to protect the women and children whom they promised peace and life. We are putting a new system that holds everyone accountable not just for their actions but for their existence as well. Your actions and your existence can make you liable to be judged under our system using international laws. Some institutions like the UNSC etc are believed to stop wars and have stated and promised people that they stop wars when in fact they can't.

New laws against misrepresenting facts and tricking people can be initiated. Giving people a false sense of protection and security only to let them be killed.

Giving a false sense of protection and security but acting as distractions so that no one stops the war.

I argued that in Tomorrow's World Order Dealing with the Threats of Invasions, Wars, and War Crimes, these institutions and cults were created by the very people who are at the forefront of wars. That makes us ask if they were created to stop wars their creators start?

Or they are there just to distract everyone else. Giving the victims a false sense of hope and a license to kill women and children. Then act to facilitate the warmongers who kill women and children. Above all give protection to those who kill women and children so that they can walk free.

Whose interests do they have? The children and the women who end up dead? Or those who founded them? The ones who start or trigger wars for resources or to offload their ever-growing weapon stockpiles and make even unfair deals at the expense of those suffering and experiencing wars.

Some cults like Nato, etc have barbaric rules, principles, articles, etc that are out of touch with reality. That is oppressive and unfair. That in the end, they fuel wars, and the use of abolished practices like slavery, torture, etc. Where other nations, based on principles like article 5 of Nato go on to breach all international laws just because they have guaranteed protection. That no matter what evil they do; they will never be accused of anything or attacked. Good or bad deeds; Nato will still protect them.

This can't be allowed.

We are not against any but all these institutions must amend their articles, principles, etc to reflect the modern times or risk being annihilated by TWO.

We are for protection based on merit. We advocate for a system where every nation, cult, institution, etc MUST abide by all international laws first. Laws are there to safeguard the continuity of humanity. Laws that have been there from the beginning of time. Laws that guarantee the existence of humanity.

We have the responsibility and obligation to do whatever it takes to make sure that there will be future generations. Just like what other previous people did to make sure we will be here on earth today.

Anyone who breaches international laws be it a country, a president, prime minister, monarchy, cult, institution or individual is answerable to us.

We are not rulers of the world, no. We are overseers, guardians, negotiators, mediators, and facilitators of human existence. It is now an undisputed consensus that some people, cults, institutions, etc through their acts of making WMDs need to be controlled for the protection of all humanity.

The reason is that the rise of technology has seen other people, nations, cults, etc recreate digital pathogens that nearly wiped-out humanity from the face of the earth. These nations, cults, etc believe that this is what real power is. This gives them, they believe, the ability to control and manipulate everyone.

We argued that this is not just plain stupidity but a crime against humanity. One we must swiftly act on.

Risks of extinction posed by never seen before concealed technologically advanced digital manmade pathogens.

We strongly believe that humanity is in danger of extinction. Due to advanced technology. We strongly believe that mankind has discovered a way to recreate all the diseases causing pathogens. And is creating digital viruses, bacteria, etc. All weapons of mass destruction [WMDs]. We believe that the current pandemic is a man-made digital one. Where a few countries are given license to commit mass murder guaranteed by article 5. Have been let to make WMDs. We believe that they are making lethal WMDs but digital versions of the pathogens. To use to gain a competitive advantage. Most countries like these believe in the divine right doctrine. They believe God or Allah put them in place to run the world. But we believe that mankind exists today because even though it faced lethal pathogens in the past, like the black death, etc even worse lethal ones. Then it was all-natural pathogens meaning that at some point.

People developed resistance to the pathogens. That alone meant some people developed immunity to the pathogens. Therefore, survived all this to safeguard the existence of humanity.

But our main concern today is that humanity is creating digital versions of the pathogens. Above all making tough strains to be sure that no one will ever be resistant to these digital pathogens. That alone is a critical factor. One that triggers our rise to the world front. As overseers, guardians, negotiators, meditators, and stewards with immediate effect. We have information that all western countries are implanting in all their people; chips, diodes, rotary propellers, etc at birth. All this in the name of medical records, etc. But we have discovered that these are the very reasons for the rise of the making of digital pathogens. Without these miniature computers, chips, rotary propellers, etc, in the name of the so-called medical record, etc. No digital pathogens will work on humans. For these digital pathogens to be able to work. They need these miniature computers or chips. Ones that are secretly implanted in all people of the developed worlds at birth.

Mankind trying to be clever and outsmart others has created and is creating lethal digital pathogens. Ones that no human being [with a computer chip etc as I said which is a requirement at birth in all developed countries] can have immunity to.

In that regard, mankind has become a threat to himself. Seeing himself as clever in creating these digital pathogens and implanting devices in all at birth. That means a potential for extinction of mankind through the making of digital pathogens that are capable of wiping all humanity.

The need for new concealed secret weapons has emphasized the need for TWO. Mankind has looked for technology to find answers to the growing anti-war movements and human rights campaigns and activists etc. This has meant that mankind looks for hidden secretive but lethal weapons, digital weapons to carry on killing others for whatever reasons. There is the use of digital weapons that use electromagnetic nerve tampering etc imitating real pathogens.

Don't believe that these don't exist. These do exist. If you think the current pandemic is biological then think again. We believe that even if the initial outbreak was biological, they used digital ones to kill as many people as they did. See the emails attached for more details.

We have raised concerns to all international institutions but to no avail.

III

Risks and potential for an all-out nuclear war that will cause the annihilation of humanity.

Secondly, the current global setting is a disaster for the existence of humanity. The fact that the current system is unbalanced, unfair, and as I argued in all my books. Already collapsed and obsolete, and the making and possession of nuclear weapons. Weapons of Mass Destruction [WMDs] are a deadly combination. One that if we don't take over will see the extinction of humanity.

Lack of a neutral negotiator to control the situation. Dangers of the in-the-heat-of-the-moment scenes. Unstable, tampered leaders with hands on the trigger of nuke warheads.

Currently, there is no one to safeguard that the countries with nukes will not use them for whatever reason. In all cases, with resulting consequences of the risk of human extinction. The current war has created the need for a new world order. The need for new neutral power. One to safeguard humanity's existence. By putting things in place to control everyone for the sake of peace, and the existence of humanity. I argued that Nato's article 5 makes everyone uneasy and worry for their protection. As it gives protection to all countries making WMDs nevertheless digital, concealed and secretly, etc. That triggers others to make even more destructive nuclear weapons. Mostly in public. This is because they know that Nato members make even worse WMDs. Nevertheless, concealed ones which make no difference to them at all.

Everyone has the right to protect themselves. I argue in Tomorrow's

World Order Dealing with the threats of invasions, wars, and war crimes; that the magnitude and threat at hand. Can trigger a nation to use WMDs like nuclear weapons as a direct proportion to the threat at hand as a self-defense mechanism.

Where the balance is overwhelmingly unbalanced e.g if Nato is to take on Russia. This can make Russia use nuclear weapons. Just because of the proportion and magnitude of the threat in Nato to Russia. Can be perceived as nothing other than requiring the use of WMDs in nukes to match.

The critical point in time that requires immediate action. The need for a new power to be involved in critical planning to implement an urgent risk strategy. To act as negotiators, containers, risk-eliminators, etc.

You can tell that the world right now is in a dangerous situation. A situation is so critical that it will be stupid and gross miscalculations if we as TWO don't take over to contain this 'nuclear bomb situation'. One surely capable of causing the extinction of mankind.

Anyone against this idea. Is against us. Is against the survival of humanity. Therefore, a Hostis Humanis Generis. An enemy of the people. One fit to be attacked by all at our commands.

The situation can get out of hand quickly and easily. This justifies our rise to the global arena as guardians, peacekeepers, etc. Critical-urgent risk management and planning have become critical requirements for the system.

No one should oppose this idea. We are neutral. Even though we are officially registered in the United Kingdom. We don't represent anyone. The two critical situations. Ones I have discussed above. Have meant the need to overhaul the current system. The need for a new setting. A New World Order. The rise of TWO.

Gone are the days when we leave things to chance. We mean business. We have powers to command all nations. To attack a leader, nation, cult, etc who breaches international laws. Anyone against what the world stands for. We have a global collective goal. To safeguard the existence of humanity and any threat to that is dealt with swiftly and harshly.

The current system only triggers further acts that can cause the extinction of humanity.

Imagine how easy it can get out of hand? How any country, not just Russia but one not a member of Nato can feel insecure knowing that Nato simply protects all evil members, etc. All are not based on their merit. Meaning even worse countries using digital technology, nevertheless concealed [weapons of mass destruction] are protected by Nato.

The current system formed after the second world war was and is there to hold-in-place the obsolete system. Where weapons are drivers of the economy. Where stockpiling and huge military budgets especially with the rise of the anti-war, human rights movements, etc. Put pressure that can see the crash of the system. Especially as the stockpiles overspill, then unless the system is controlled the system will crash. I argued in Tomorrow's World Order that Nato, UNSC, UN, etc were put in place to prevent the collapse of the system meaning to just hold-it-in-place.

Imagine if Nato, UN, UNSC, etc did not exist. If or didn't have article 5, etc then the international law would prevail. No member country or anyone would make WMD secretly e.g, digital ones like the pandemic. Everyone would be afraid enough to make nukes. It is easy in this case to believe that all will abide by international laws.

Above all, international laws would prohibit the making of WMDs in the interest of the continuation of human existence. No country would break these laws without paying the price. International law would prevail whether a Nato member or not. That would make no difference.

Most institutions; like human rights bodies, etc would challenge and bring to justice successfully, any country that breaks these laws.

Lawyers, human rights activists, etc would have the power to stop all this. But this is not the case, Nato, UNSC, etc give blanket immunity to members. To their founders, the very countries at the forefront of wars, sanctions, etc.

Therefore Nato, UNSC, UN's, etc, presence is to safeguard lawbreakers. Protect all and give license to continue with evil. To such an extent that another member country feels omnipotent that it is led to believe in the divine right. That only God can judge it.

We have advocated for Nato, to give protection based on merits. Meaning protecting only member nations that abide by international laws. Also, to be involved in denouncing those who breach these laws. But don't forget that Nato, UNSC, etc were created by the very countries at the forefront of wars or triggering wars and all human rights abuses.

In law, using traditional hooding as a means of torture or using a digital version of hooding. One where a chip and rotary propeller are implanted at birth for so-called protection or medical records. Then these are used to rotate the eye's iris at an angle into the eye socket, and that vision is lost. These are all hooding; the same methods of torture. So, a country that uses the method openly and an advanced country that does the same; digitally are all equal.

It is not whether it can be proved or not; as the current thinking.

There is therefore a need for a neutral world leader in us; TWO, to act as the referee. To act as the guardian force, the guarding principle, the overseers, and the negotiator between disputing countries.

The current system's setting can only fuel wars and inequalities. Above all, this is so critical as this imbalance of the status quo to an extent that can trigger the extinction of humanity. The reason why I emphasized much on the west, Nato, UN, UNSC, etc is that they believe that they have powers to stop wars, protect the people, and be the world leaders. To act in the interest of all etc but is that so?

1. Does Nato with its members in the USA, UK, Europe, etc represent everyone's interest?

2. Do Nato members etc represent all non-white countries etc?

3. Do Nato's members represent the political, religious, social, and financial interests of all people in the world?

Or I should ask if Nato is different from the 1980's gangsters, or cults? Ones who only look after their members regardless of whether their members abide by all international laws or not.

Is Nato different from gangsters who send their smallest member to rob, burglar, and murder other nations, etc whatever the reason they give makes no difference?

All this, with Nato waiting to see who of those who were burgled are to complain to them. Then instead, further attack the victims who got burglarized using Article 5 to protect the thieving-smallest-member.

Is Nato aware that member nations breach all international laws? Were they made aware that their members are breaching international laws? What actions did they take? Did they denounce these nations? Or it's just blanket protection regardless of these breaches of international law.

Take the UNSC; which states that they stop wars. Do they stop wars? In any sense of the phrase or word? Can they stand in court and declare that to the women and children who end up dead and who do believe that they stop wars? In most cases, the ones who end up dead? In their capacity are they in a position to stop wars? Do they have a framework that stops wars? Above all can they stop wars that their founders and funders have started? Can they stop wars that their founders have indirectly triggered? In that article 5 is a blanket protection to culprits that makes others embark on wars to protect themselves?

Can they stop wars that fund them directly? I argued in my book Tomorrow's World Order that UNSC cannot fight their founders who fund them. The settings make it impossible to stand up to wars.

One might argue that this time it [current war] was not started by a Nato member as it was triggered by Russia. True. But the UNSC, etc are biased and work in Nato's interest. They are part of the West's system of holding-in-place the already collapsed system. So, any intervention by UNSC would have seen Russia get all-raged up. This is as good as the west sending their smallest member to do bad things just for them to see who complains and for them to use article 5 to attack the complainer. In any way a trigger of wars.

IV

The current Predicament.

The current system and all institutions like the UN, and UNSC that declares to stop wars. Are all biased, in the way they were founded and formed. Further inclination to whose interests they represent make them unfit to stop wars. Either way, there was going to be mistrust, etc, anyway. The system, as I argued in all my books, is designed to be a defensive system. That forever will have wars and weapons as drivers of the economy. As long as the system is there forever there will be a war. Resources are plowed into the military instead of in search of alternative resources. Like solar electricity or other fuels. That forever will slow progress into research into other energy fuel processes. The huge investments into the military cause a multiplier effect in that the insecurity and mistrust by other countries, cults, etc increase too.

Our main concern is that if left to chance. This will trigger a huge third world war where everyone will use nuclear weapons. This is because of the threat at hand which will be enormous. Justifying the use of even more lethal weapons.

So, it is fate and imminent for Tomorrow's World Order to take over as the new global readers. We have everyone's interest at heart. We command all military, institutions, cults, individuals, nations, etc.

The legal international court system like every system was created, founded, and is funded by the countries either at the forefront of wars. Or ones that are fuelling mistrust in the system and wars.

Above all, they can't stop wars, as they were formed only to deal with the aftermath of wars. They are given existence and purpose by wars. So unlikely to stop wars. Imagine courts that judge people before they commit crimes? On what basis can this be proved especially on their reliance on evidence etc. That means without wars they would stop existing. That explains why they never stop wars but negotiate for peace after wars have started. After women and children have died.

Most, even if a country breaches international law and acknowledges it. All it can do is offer an advisory judgment that is useless and not enforceable.

Above all like all systems are funded by the same countries and cults behind all injustices.

Again article 5 takes over. The man with the gun becomes the prevailing law. As international law is broken by member states and nevertheless Nato still protects these member states.

All institutions like the UNSC act as distractors to give the victims a false sense of security. So as not to act or show increased fear [A self-preservation attribute.] etc that makes them escape before the war starts. The reason is to make the object of their masters. Ones who trigger wars. Be met within a short period and with less effort. In most cases exonerate the killers of women and children by shifting the blame from the killers to themselves. Also, to create a situation that justifies their existence. Making only refugees run war zones when the wars have begun. Stealing the time of the victims. Imagine if all refugees can escape weeks before wars. There won't be a scene that justifies e.g, condemnation of the wars by the UN, etc. But picture condemnations that are made as people are trapped as a direct result of the war. They have more impact on them.

Obsolete Useless Institutions.

Not trying to be fun. I mentioned in my book that the current system was established just after the second world war. A system that is honestly obsolete in that they have to keep recreating the conditions when they were established. Meaning as in the case of hospitals, etc making digital pathogens to keep them viable and have a sense of existence. I argued that advances in health, etc have meant no need for hospitals as it was then. Now, these evils are deliberately recreating all the diseases and pathogens that have been eradicated replacing these with digital ones. Making them viable in turn.

The greatest risk to humanity's survival is brought by the development of digital tough strain pathogens.

The real danger and the trigger of our rise as TWO is to keep viable and not to go obsolete. They are making strong strains of digital pathogens that no human can resist. Be very careful about this digital chipping of people in the name of medical records. If let to do this, these institutions, etc will cause the extinction of humanity. I argued that we as humans survived only because some people developed resistance to different pathogens over centuries. Ending up with a better version of humanity that withstands all pathogens. This is the very reason that pandemics don't occur as much and as lethal as in the past centuries, etc. This with improved technology and medicine has meant obsoletion of some institutions. That they have begun illegally implanting everyone [especially in the developed world] with an electrode diode and a rotary propeller to use electromagnetic nerve tampering which makes it possible to recreate digital pathogens and disease etc.

This means a new world order is imminent to stop humanity from self-destruction.

V

Factors that made the rise of TWO mandatory.

The heightened risk of making more and more lethal intercontinental nuclear weapons as technology improves.

The world is stuck in the defensive stage of development. Strong habits die hard. There is a need for a new global leader to take mankind out of the defensive stage.

I argue that nature since the beginning of time has put things in places like wars, famine, and all-natural disasters as catalysts to change and help humanity to move forward through the development stages. See Tomorrow's World Order for the stages of development.

Wars as triggers for the evolution of mankind. The move to other stages of development.

I argued that wars were meant for mankind to feel the pain first then pain open their eyes to see the evils that wars bring and then abandon wars never to fight again. Then never make bombs that cause so much suffering. As a natural trigger for development and evolutionary progress to the next stage. Wars as fate were meant to make mankind move to the next stage of development. A move from the defensive stage. A stage where weapons are paramount and drivers of the economy. To a stage of technological development where technology is the driver of the economy.

If the current system was not put in place after the second world war. Naturally and as an imminent event. Humans would have inevitably abandoned wars, less emphasized weapons manufacturing {nevertheless through experiencing the war traumas} this should have propelled him to the next stage of networking. Where they invest heavily in technology.

But then {in 1945} the trauma of seeing wars made mankind put things in place to cushion himself from wars. Naturally, the war trauma would have been forgotten after two years.

The problem here is that mankind only thought for that period just after WWII and not for the long run by creating Nato, UN, UNSC, etc. Before this time wars occurred after a certain period roughly twenty years in-between with WWI having occurred twenty years before that. Another war will have occurred twenty years later during the 1960s evidenced by the 1960 cold war. This was to be a war to end all wars. A war to propel mankind to give up weapons and move into networking and cooperation.

This is our main concern in that even though mankind thinks he is smart and has solved the problems associated with wars. He has jammed the system in the defensive stage. A dangerous stage where weapons and military take a huge chunk of the budget. Picture a driver who jams a car gear system in first gear just before entering the motorway? Can you see what can go wrong? This is what humanity has done. Stuck and if we don't take over; humanity is doomed for extinction. Simply because more and more dangerous weapons will be made continuously and with everyone just stockpiling these. This means huge tensions as well. As other areas suffer to an extent that even Nato which is there to suppress human rights activists, complainers, etc. Will not be able to contain the tension without triggering a world nuclear war.

This is proof: nuclear warheads by country 2022.

Russia 5977

USA 5428

UK 225

China 350

North Korea 50

France 290

Ask yourself. Where would these nuclear warheads end up? Is this not a recipe for disaster? An accident waiting to happen

But war pain is meant to be the driver of mankind to move forward as the effects of wars. Of which the war trauma lasts only two years after that it would be easy to forget and move forward. But mankind put things in place within the two years in fact just after WWII, with one aim, intending to hold-in-place the already crashed system. Mind you, wars, etc are proof of a system crash. An imbalance exists, as resources are plowed into the military at the expense of technology or human welfare. This can only result in some kind of tension and revolt.

What mankind did by putting things to hold-in-place the already crashed system, was to jam everything so that mankind is stuck in the defensive stage. A stage we have been in since the second world war. Okay, that helped stop wars but created a ticking-time-bomb.

I explained in my book that wars have cycles of occurrence if wrong allocations of resources occurred. To correct this, the war would follow to correct the effect. The first world war was such a war. Then came the second world war. If the current system was not put in place there would have been a third World War. We will see to it that mankind abandons weapons and moves out of the defensive stage to a stage of networking and technological advancement. I am not saying that there were not going to be wars ever again. But I am saying we would have new forms of wars brought by the advancement in technology. Technological wars instead. So now we have been stuck in the defensive stages.

VI

How do we solve this current mess?

There are two solutions to deal with this manmade current problem. Mankind jammed everything in place to prevent wars. So that there won't be change as long as the current system is in place.

The first solution is to remove all the things put in place to hold-in-place the obsolete, already crashed system. This means the destruction of the current system, removal of Nato, UN, UNSC, IMF, World Bank, etc. The jammers of the move to a new better-advanced system of human development.

The problems are that membership conditions are simply based on article 5 instead of on merit in relation to international laws' obedience. If it was on merit then humanity would still progress to the next stage of development. Would progress to the next stage of development, simply because human rights defenders etc would point to the injustices. This could have triggered a war to change things forever. So, the war would have been inevitable.

The current system causes the grouping of nations with the same thinking as one but since it's a system there will be equally opposing forces who forever would disagree. The greater the grouping into cults like Nato the greater the chance of others making WMDs in response to the force and threat at hand. Hence the risk to humanity's survival as WMDs might be used by both sides. If Russia is cornered, for example, it might use a nuclear warhead in self-defense. Or as in the Hiroshima justification; to shorten the war.

Should we allow this to happen? Or not put a contingency plan to counteract the possibility of this happening?

Hence the need for an immediate global power that is neutral and fair to act as referees, overseers, guardians, etc. Hence the rise of TWO.

But face reality there is no way UN, UNSC, NATO, World Bank, IMF, etc are just going to stop existing. Instead, they are going to grow even bigger. As Russia etc threatens a nuclear war they are to match the threat as well. Now Russia is regarded as a bigger threat because of the number of nuclear warheads. So according to them that justifies the making of WMDs.

This is a vicious cycle that triggers the ever growing number of nuclear warheads. A real threat to the existence of mankind.

The fact that there are more countries. If not, all countries are involved in this. This means the urgent requirement of a new world order with us as the new leaders. Imagine Nato members and other countries like Russia, China, India, etc, and all Arab countries all using nuclear weapons? Then who will be left after the nuclear war if they are all involved? Hence the need for us to stop this before it escalates to uncontrollable levels. The first option of leaving things to chance is unworkable. Simply because of the institutions, cults, etc that are now jamming the movement to another stage of development. That means we need interveners to control the jammers {Nato, UN, UNSC, IMF, World Bank, etc} which we regard as landmines, grenades, etc. Those are there but ones that must be carefully made safe first. To stop them from exploding and killing everyone. Then safely make them safe for all. This brings me to the second option.

VII

WE CAN'T LEAVE THINGS TO CHANCE.

We rose to fill the huge gap in the current global justice system. The pandemic and the current war have highlighted serious critical shortfalls of the current system, especially in terms of defending women and children who end up dead due to wars. In stopping wars. In negotiating or in the provision of such a framework. In support of people who need assistance at a time of need, among other things.

The Heightened Risks Of Human Extinction.

Intensified risk and actual use of Weapons of Mass Destruction [WMDs] brought by advanced technological advancement nevertheless concealed digital WMDs are being used and the political climate where Nato's article 5 gives immunity to countries breaking international laws regarding weapons of mass destruction.

Nato's expansion and their blanket protection to all kinds of evil using article 5 and the intense political climate where other countries have to match the force and threat at hand in Nato led them to make even more destructive weapons in nukes. The current war is proof of how thin a line it is between extinction and humanity's survival.

Tomorrow's World Order
Official Strategic Launch
www.twocoming.com
tomorrowsworldorder@outlook.com
00447745900178

To:

The Russian and Ukrainian Governments

Mr Presidents

STOP THE WAR NOW.

Only you two have the power to do so.

We are deeply concerned with the huge loss of lives. As a matter of urgency and emergency, we call for the **immediate cessation of the conflict, loss of lives, deteriorating humanitarian situation, and the immediate start of negotiations in order to reach a peaceful and lasting soluti**on.

The good news is that there is a solution to the conflict. Through us, you can start immediate negotiations that lead to peace. We provide a platform and environment for peace and sound fruitful negotiations that lead to diplomatic, sustainable resolutions.

We are the new global leaders, peacekeepers, negotiators, mediators, facilitators, and defenders of the defenceless mainly women and children, among other things.

We strongly believe that the lack of a proper plaftorm to encourage dialogue, diplomacy, negotiations and the mistrust of the current system is the sole reason why this escalated into this conflict.

We know the system is not what it seems. The current system is broken, dysfunctional and honestly not fit for purpose. Surely we strongly believe that if proper channels of negotiations were available. Channels trusted by both of you Mr Presidents. Surely the conflict could have been resolved in a diplomatic way through dialogue.

We therefore take this opportunity to introduce a new world order that means peace for all.

There is hope for an amicably diplomatic resolution to the conflict.

We therefore require the immediate cessation of this conflict and the immediate cessation of hostilities and the immediate start of dialogue without any preconditions.

You must fully comply with our requirements for we stand for all.

We are neutral and represent all humanity.

We know the current system let you all down but there is hope. We are the future. It is not too late to reach a peaceful and lasting solution to the crisis.

START PEACE NEGOTIATIONS WITH IMMEDIATE EFFECT DIPLOMACY IS THE ONLY SOLUTION.

signed President Tomorrow's World Order 24 April 2022 David Gomadza.

VIII

Part II

The main reason why I concentrated mostly on the West is the fact that if we are to face resistance. It will be from this side. This is because the west considers itself the global leader and believes they are acting in everyone's best interest. But this is just a fantasy. We have proved that they don't represent anyone but their interests only. No matter how harsh this might sound. The world is not the west. The world has changed. Gone are the days when bully gangsters, cults, send their smallest members to rob, burglar, and kill others with them just waiting to see who complains after all this, etc. Then sanction all. Stealing wealth from the hard-working people etc, the others mostly the victims of wets policies see them no less like 1980s gangster thieves who use weapons to steal at gunpoint. Then impose sanctions to kill women and children to bring their enemies to the negotiating table.

All this no matter how unbelievable this might sound. Is triggered by article 5 which protects all members regardless of their merit vis a vis the international laws.

It is a fact that most enemies of the west are countries that are now arming themselves with nukes in response to the force and threat at hand in Nato. Most of these are fearful and as a means of self-defense now arm themselves. Despite all this cannot equal the force and threat at hand as Nato expands and grows.

All those in the east would rather see an intermediator, a negotiator, and a power they can complain to, a power neutral to all these differences. A power to judge the fairness of the system and put a platform to neutralize the tensions between the west and the east.

The east is welcome to a new world order as the current system disadvantages them. In most cases, they consider themselves as victims but blessed to possess minerals, etc. The west lacks mineral resources. They believe that the imbalance is the trigger of all the wars. They, therefore, believe that they created this system to redistribute resources equally and to control others for peace purposes. But in the process kill women and children in the name of peace.

Therefore, people in the east welcome a new global power they consider to be fair and just. One to act as a just judge.

It's not a crime not to have the resources which one needs or the ability to pay a fair market price for scarce resources. The reasons why cults etc were put in place is to get the resources without wars. Or to take through wars, sanctions, and all kinds of evil.

We, as TWO, believe that mismanagement and ineffective priorities are now the big issues rather than the distribution of the resources, etc. Nature would have triggered the move from the defensive stage of development to a new stage of networking and cooperation. After the realization, that man's greatest enemy is mankind himself. That would have freed resources from the military for the development of alternative sources of energy and fuel. But the current system, one put in place, means the military eats away funds that would otherwise be used to develop alternate fuels, etc.

The bigger the number of countries joining Nato, etc, the more the threat levels. If raised to the highest levels. The greater the imbalance and risk of an all-out- nuclear weapons war.

So, we must take over with immediate effect. I can't stress enough how important we are right now. Especially after the pandemic which we believe was man-made and the current war and the risks of a nuclear war.

All these have defied the existence of humanity as threats levels have been raised to the highest levels ever. There was no risk of an all-out nuclear war ever more than now.

We don't need anyone's permission to take over as the new world leaders but this makes us sure that everyone knows there is a new law and order in town.

This does not mean that the east, etc are innocent and have victims' status, etc, no. It is only that they are not as advanced as the west. Ones who are clever use technology to hide and conceal their atrocities through the use of digital technology. Nevertheless, doing the same by recreating all that which the east is doing is only hidden and secretly. Hacking all children at birth by implanting chips since the end of the second world war. The east is to blame too. The east argues that the west's system protects even worse culprits; countries who break all international laws and get away with it. They believe that until the west has been brought to justice there is no point to point at them. Simply because the west is no angel and is not in a position to tell anyone what is wrong or right.

That makes us the only fair system. We have no vested interests in wars, sanctions, human rights abuses, etc.

In the east when they carry out human rights abuses, they go to extremes. But that does not mean that the west is an angel. The west, as I pointed out in my books, uses concealed sophisticated technology to do worse. Where people can complain and if they do no one believes them as they are classed as hallucinating.

So, the west hides its abuses by labeling ethnic minorities as hallucinating. Anyone who complains is hallucinating. Therefore, you will notice high cases of people regarded as hallucinating, etc in the west as compared to eastern countries. Also, high rates of human rights abuses in the east where they use primitive methods of torture, etc. The other reason that justifies our rise to power is the fact that women and children are abused by both the west and the east.

The west kills women through sanctions and wars to make their enemies quickly end the struggle and come to the negotiating table years before they invaded.

That means they use the women's and children's deaths as ways of reducing the length of the war and the casualties they might suffer themselves. It is a fact we have proved that sanctions are intended to kill women and children as they originated with the scorched earth policy. Tactics that are used to remove any support the enemy can get.

That means the east uses children and women for cover. Putting women and children in front of them with the belief that the west won't attack and kill them. But this is not what happens for example as a strategic plan, to weaken enemies and shorten the war with the west beforehand, sanction countries years before the time they will attack as part of the strategic plan. To weaken and remove any form of protection from their enemies by using women and children as bargaining tools.

We as TWO don't care why they do it. We are saying that they all let women and children die easily and unnecessarily without anyone brought to justice. This is a gross miscarriage of justice. Hence, we must safeguard the lives of women and children who are the victims.

The east looks to the so-called international institutions like the UNSC to stop wars but to their disbelief, they realize that they can't stop wars. We have explained why that is so; read other books. One characteristic of the east is sectoral violence. Wars between people who have similar backgrounds etc all, because of land, religion, divisions, etc, or other resources. Russian and Ukraine war falls into this category of a war between nations close together who share similar identities, backgrounds, beliefs, etc over territorial beliefs, etc.

A war if just between the two might not be regarded as a risk to the survival of and existence of humanity. But the current circumstances with Nato willing to protect others mostly members no matter at what cost is the risk to the survival of humanity. That has turned a territorial dispute into a potential human extinction threat.

IX

Our stance as TWO

All in my books I appear to be strict with the west rather than the east. But trust me there is no bias. The west declares itself as the global leader. One serving everyone's interests. Standing for justice and human rights. But if you consider the fact that they have just shifted to the use of concealed technologically advanced methods of doing the same as the east. Declaring things like slavery, torture, etc as abolished only after discovering concealed secret digital versions of the same methods the east used openly then you will understand.

Even worse is the fact that they have article 5 that gives all muggers, murderers, torturers, etc blanket protection then you will understand why we are this strict with the west.

Also, the fact that to us they give people a false sense of security. They declare they do things that give people hope only for them not to react and for the people to end up dead.

I think this carries more scrutiny and punishment. Just because they immobilize the victims who if they did not give them that false sense of protection. The people would run as survival instincts kick in. It's tricking people especially in the case of the UNSC. They must be dragged to court and punished.

If they can't stop wars, they must cease to exist.

Who better to tell them than Zelensky.

"If there is no alternative and no option, then the next option would be to dissolve yourself altogether," Zelenskyy said.

Addressing the United Nations Security Council.

This is a crime itself of impersonating a war stopper. Tough laws must be used to destroy all these using compensations to victims' relatives to bankrupt all.

The east doesn't give that false sense of hope and security. Wars in their countries are characterized by a huge outflux of migrants before wars start. We believe it's the west's tactic to avoid refugee influx etc and above all to avoid critics criticizing the war with such acts regarded as strategic objectives or special military excess. So that it's regarded as normal to look as if these are acts within the laws etc.

I believe the world expected Nato to act as peacekeepers. Enter or send forces just to keep Russians out but was surprised they did not. Why?

Nato has intervened in the past not to fight but to provide protection as a peace entity. The fact that they do not intervene means they have good reasons to do that. They believe that the risks are high. That also means something [TWO] must be in place. If Nato is scared to protect Ukraine's people from dying, that means there is a gap somewhere. A gap we must fill as TWO. Everyone hoped for them to intervene and then even win Ukraine's people who would have joined Nato after the rescue. Would you not if in their shoes?

The risk of unsettling or frightening Russia can culminate into a real nuclear global war.

Nato knows this and I believe they will not have issues with us becoming intermediators, negotiators, and facilitators.

Hence our concerns that we must take over with immediate effect. This means the risks are greater that Nato would let people in Ukraine be killed. They know the consequence would be greater if Russia is to retaliate with nukes in retaliation to Nato's force and threat at hand.

You must all acknowledge us as Tomorrow's World Order. We have a bigger role to play just like everyone else. We are the missing link. We will modernize the system and neutralize the tensions.

Are you ready for us?

We have British citizens on the team. We have Latvians, Lithuanians, Romanians, Polish, Africans, Asians, etc on the team. We stand for the whole world. You all MUST appreciate what we will bring to this dysfunctional obsolete system. You need us.

We have rights to our fiat currency.

I am the Global President and Founder: David Gomadza

President Europe: Bogdan Gavrila

President Europe & Great Britain: Carolina Zeiberlina

President Raj Ali Great Britain & Middle East.

President Africa: Isaiah Mudzimu

Are we better than the current system, the UNSC, UN, etc who declare they stop wars without any means to do so?

Firstly, we understand the system better as we are neutral, we will represent everyone's interest and therefore become better judges, negotiators, facilitators, etc.

We will have a military wing; an enforcing wing and tough laws. Our system is based on the idea of the Hostis Humanis Generis notion that anyone who poses a threat to the existence of humanity is regarded as an enemy of the people. One who deserves to be attacked by the whole world.

We might not have the military capabilities of all militaries like Nato but we have the international law and the need to protect humanity from a few people who take the law into their own hands.

Our system believes in the fact that with us. The law is an individual thing. each person stands by himself judged by his actions in relation to the existence of humanity. Meaning leaders who pose a risk to humanity's survival through the commanding of the making of digital pathogens or nukes [all WMDs] can be blasted by their members, in the name of preserving humanity.

We are to take advantage of the technological development that at one point we will use thoughts and dreams to command people to carry out our tasks. So don't be complacent. Better stay away from breaching international laws. We are developing advanced technological methods that use thoughts, inner voice, dreams, etc to talk, command, etc. Read Thoughts to Word or Audio and Decoding Thoughts and inner voice.

We will give commands through dreams and thoughts. So be careful you don't want to be on the wrong side of international law.

Our stance on invasions etc is that no matter what. No sovereign country can be invaded. We will put things in place to see that it is so. We shall have a stronghold of 200 assassins to enforce our laws. We believe that TWO is for us all but one man or woman for himself or herself. This is the only way individuals' acts are to make them be held accountable.

X

A New World Order.

I know it's a long road but we must start somewhere.

The current war happened so fast even though we anticipated a war this year we didn't expect it this soon. We warmed Nato etc that life is not what it seems. Some countries have become so manipulative using a system that collects information in such a way that every year they recreate a period in the past. Putting lookalikes then replay what happened then. The main reason is that they want to have a competitive advantage. Imagine knowing what is going to happen all over the world in the future? Or the crash of financial markets in the future? That information could be vital.

A New World Order.

Is needed to offset the current state of things. To break the cycle and change the course of events.

Looking at the current war I think not asking the right questions can leave the leader of a country to be liable and to be accountable to us especially if many people end up dead. Not doing enough in terms of asking for international help can leave someone liable to us.

I argued that a sovereign nation is automatically protected by international laws. In that, a leader of that country can ask for the international community to come to help them. Anyone whom he asks for help is obliged to help without fear of what the invader is capable of doing.

Failure is a crime under our laws. If you can't carry out your international duties to safeguard a sovereign nation then stop existing.

I mention that failure constitutes a crime. In cases like this, you have an obligation to push invaders out and keep them out at whatever expense. The rule changes only if the country being attacked or being invaded has broken international laws itself.

In this case, the invading nations would be punishing the country due to their breaches of international laws. Was this the case in this war?

UN, UNSC, Nato's, etc refusal to deal with shutting down the air space alone might constitute a crime if women and children went on to be killed.

Refusal to provide foot soldiers if asked by a sovereign country can constitute a crime if women and children went on to die.

Arming civilians can constitute a crime as well if many end up dead as this might remove the protection civilians have under international laws. Once armed a civilian loses the civilian privileges not to be killed in wars. Some can argue that civilians have become soldiers. A kid with a gun and able to use it is different from an unarmed kid who ends up dead. But that is why we must take over and establish what is what with wars going forward.

If you are serious about peace and a better world. Then welcome to Tomorrow's World Order.

We will cover pressing issues in the next book.

We are the defenders of women and children who might die because of wars.

We stand with any victims of wars.

We stand against all wars.

We stand against invasions of sovereign countries.

We believe in the right to defend oneself.

We believe in the upholding of all international laws that safeguard humanity.

We are against the use of weapons of mass destruction be it nuclear or digital viruses.

We stand for global peace.

We stand for all.

The death of a child or a woman is an attack on all of us.

We believe in the power of negotiations and peace talks.

We believe in dialogue first.

We believe in exhausting all avenues of peace first.

We are against weapons and the making of weapons.

We must be the intermediators, negotiators, and channels of communication between disputing nations.

We must be the first contacts in a dispute.

A better world for all.

A brand new system of global governance.

WELCOME TO TOMORROW@S WORLD ORDER

Signed

24 April 2022

David Gomadza

Founder and President

Tomorrow's World Order

www.twocoming.com

Tomorrowsworldorder@outlook.com

00447745900178

ABOUT DAVID GOMADZA

President and Founder of Tomorrow's World Order

Project Leader, CEO and Founder of Gtps.Finance

I have written several books, see links below or simply search for David Gomadza.

MUST READ.

Tomorrow's World Order.

https://play.google.com/store/books/details/David_Gomadza_Tomorrow_s_World_Order?id=VDauDwAAQBAJ

Tomorrow's World Order. Dealing with the threats of invasion, wars, and war crimes.

https://play.google.com/store/books/details/David_Gomadza_Tomorrow_s_World_Order_A_New_Law_Ord?id=ws3ODwAAQBAJ

Tomorrow's World Order's Sovsuperiuscogens

https://play.google.com/store/books/details/David_Gomadza_Tomorrow_s_World_Order_s_Sovsuperius?id=fT--DwAAQBAJ

The Constitution Tomorrow's World Order

https://play.google.com/store/books/details/David_Gomadza_THE_CONSTITUTION_Tomorrow_s_World_Or?id=S-69DwAAQBAJ